THE CHAMPAGNE DIET

Eat, Drink & Celebrate

Your Way to A Healthy Mind and Body

CARA ALWILL LEYBA

Passionista PUBLISHING

THE CHAMPAGNE DIET

Passionista
PUBLISHING

This book is for every girl who has allowed her weight to define her as a person. You are worth so much more than a number on the scale and you are more beautiful than you will ever know.

CONTENTS

INTRODUCTION

Did Somebody Say Champagne Diet?

Di·et /'dī-it/
Something used, enjoyed, or provided regularly

Let's get something straight. This is not a diet book. I am not here to tell you how to lose weight – though I will give you fair warning; that may be a delicious added bonus as a result of our work together. This book is not about drinking champagne all day and getting skinny (oh, but wouldn't that be *glorious*?). I am not a weight-loss guru or a fitness expert.

What I am here to do is teach you how to get healthy – emotionally and physically. I'm going to teach you how to fall in love with your body at any size. I'm going to show you that you can enjoy the things you love (like champagne!) and still be healthy. I'm going to help you figure out what's getting in the way of treating yourself and your body with the love and respect it deserves – because it all starts there.

This book is for the woman who wants to feel good about herself and her body, and learn how to start incorporating healthy habits into her life. It's for the woman who doesn't want to trade in her champagne for skinny jeans. It's for the woman who is done with dieting, and ready to start paying attention to her health before that number on the scale. It's for the woman

1

who is ready to stop letting her weight define her, and is ready to understand why it always did.

This is not a diet book. This is a *lifestyle guide*.

Think about how many diet books you've read. Some of them may have been bad, some decent, and some even good – in theory. Perhaps you lost some weight, developed a new habit, or learned how to "treat your diet like a bank account." You may have even lost some weight, temporarily. But where are you now?

Hear me out, ladies: *diets do not work*. There is no amount of points, frozen dinners, calorie-counting methods, fitness apps, or fat-free cookies in the world that will make you a healthy person. Why? Because diets don't deal with your emotions.

So what is *The Champagne Diet*, exactly? It's a way of living: a diet for your mind, body, and soul that is focused on the best of the best. It means indulging in the best, healthiest foods, as well as the best, healthiest life. If you've read my book *Sparkle*, then you know how I feel about champagne. Champagne is a sexy, magical drink that creates a sense of excitement, deservedness, and happiness when it's served. It's about indulgence and decadence. And that is exactly what your lifestyle should be like.

Hear me out, ladies: diets do not work. There is no amount of points, frozen dinners, calorie-counting methods, fitness apps, or fat-free cookies in the world that will make you a healthy person Why? Because diets don't deal with your emotions.

Now, don't go running out to Mickey D's just yet. When I say decadence, I don't mean gorging on value meals and twenty-ounce Cokes – there is a huge difference. Being on The Champagne Diet means eating high-quality, nutritious foods that look sexy on your plate. It's about taking the time to think about what you're putting in your body and making sure it will serve your health first and foremost. It's about cooking a delicious meal while sipping on a glass of wine in an outfit you feel glamorous in, as opposed to heating up a diet pizza in ratty pajamas (don't act like you haven't been there). It's about paying attention to your emotions and figuring out why you ever ate those diet pizzas in the first place. You get my drift.

By this point you're probably thinking, who are you and why are you writing this? Aside from being a lifestyle and wellness coach, I'm an average woman, just like you. I've been on all the same diets. I've cried while stuffing myself into a pair of jeans. I've called myself fat more times than I can count. I've blamed my failed relationships on my weight. I've blamed my failed business endeavors on my weight. I've blamed my own unhappiness on my weight. But ultimately I got to a place where I learned to shift my focus, and I wound up so much happier and healthier than I ever imagined possible. And I'm going to teach you how to do the same.

I want you to write down the first three things that immediately come to mind when you think about your experiences with dieting and weight loss:

1. _____
2. _____
3. _____

Now, I want you to write down how you'd feel if you never had to think about your weight again:

1. _____
2. _____
3. _____

Hold those last three feelings close to you and focus on them as you read this book. They are going to be our guiding star. This book will change the way you view your weight and yourself forever. You will walk away feeling empowered, inspired, and downright sexy (and probably really in love with champagne). You will learn how to celebrate yourself and your body. You will learn to make your health a priority, always. And most importantly – you will learn to love yourself, exactly as you are. So get ready for a complete dieting and lifestyle overhaul, sister. You are now on *The Champagne Diet*!

CHAPTER ONE
Are You Worth It?

Well, duh. Of course I think you're worth it. But do you? As we embark on *The Champagne Diet*, the first thing I'm going to need you to do is truly and genuinely believe that you deserve the life of your dreams.

What do I mean by that, exactly? Allow me to let you in on the biggest secret nobody in the diet industry tells you: unless you truly believe that you deserve an amazing life, you will never, ever be successful at eating well and being healthy, and ultimately, losing weight. Unless you create a beautiful world filled with all of the things you love, you will never make positive changes in your life that lead you to love yourself and your body.

Living the "life of your dreams" can mean so many different things depending on who you talk to. For me, my "dream life" means being healthy, happy, and getting to work on my business while being surrounded by all of the things I love: my husband, my adorable little shih tzu, and my cozy apartment decorated exactly the way I like. It means loving my body and wearing clothes that make me feel my most beautiful. It means cooking at least two meals every single day. It also means winding down at night with a delicious glass or two of wine or champagne by candlelight (candlelight is my instant peace, by the way). That dream life is my reality. Why? Because I believed I deserved it all, and I designed my world to be exactly what I wanted. Believe me, I have longer-term goals, too (hello, beach house!), but for now, this feels perfect for me.

What does *your* dream life look like? Are you living it right now? Close to it? Write down what your dream life means to you. It can be as grandiose as you want, or it can be something that you feel you can achieve within the next few months.

The more you visualize that life, the closer you will get to it. I am a huge Law of Attraction gal and I have experienced first-hand how visualization works. If you can see it, it can and will be yours. I've practiced it in every area of my life: my career, my relationships, my health – all of it. So start visualizing, sister. And remember, no dream is too silly or unattainable.

So, I'm going to ask you again: are you worth it? Do you honestly think you deserve all the happiness, love and success in the world? Take a moment to really answer that. It's a tough one. In fact, I've had a few clients break down in full-on tears when I present them with that question. But that's what I'm here for. And regardless of your answer, we're going to work on getting you to a place where you feel so swaddled with love that by the end of this book, when I ask you the question again, you won't even flinch.

Unless you truly believe that you deserve an amazing life, you will never, ever be successful at eating well and being healthy, and ultimately, losing weight.

Let Go

Sometimes we don't believe we're worth it because we've been told for so long that we aren't. I know I personally dealt with a few unsupportive and downright mean people in my life who made me feel like my weight was standing in the way of me ever having a great life. Take for example, kids in middle school who taunted me for years about being chubby. I remember one kid, in particular, who called me a blimp in the seventh grade. His words were so harsh, and they stuck with me until I was about thirty years old. Or the guy who yelled "Get out of the way, you fat bitch!" as I made my way across a busy street one morning when I was at my heaviest. After flipping him the bird and calling him an "old, bald, lonely motherfucker," I went upstairs into the bathroom at work and cried my eyes out. Was it the classiest response? No, especially in the middle of Times Square, but what can I say? He struck a nerve.

Perhaps you've been through a similar experience. Maybe it was your mother or father who called you chunky growing up. Or maybe it was a former boyfriend who told you that he didn't want to have sex with you anymore because you were too fat. Aside from hoping he rots in hell (because he should), let's start to work on the one thing that is the absolute hardest to do in these situations: forgiveness. Being able to forgive people for poisoning us with horrible thoughts about our self is not easy, but it's essential in moving past the hurt and insecurities. So take a moment and think about that person (or people) who played a part in you feeling like you don't deserve amazing things, and offer them a collective "I forgive you." You may stutter before you can get it out, or roll your eyes while saying it, but the sooner you say it, the sooner we can move on and start building back up that precious self-esteem that you're going to need to truly live *The Champagne Diet.*

A Quick Guide to Kicking Your Own Ass

As we go through this book, I'm going to be your partner in crime, calling you out on your bullshit and giving you a gentle kick in the buns when necessary. I'm going to educate you, challenge you, and push you to be better. But unfortunately, you can't keep me in your back pocket for those times when you need some on-the-spot coaching (but wouldn't that be so cute? Each time you whipped me out you'd hear that sound effect of sparkles flying through the air!). But because I'm not four inches tall, you're going to have to learn the art of kicking your own ass.

What does that mean, exactly? Developing a sense of self-worth is no easy feat, especially if you've spent years biting your tongue and hiding your body. My goal is to arm you with the tools necessary for slapping some sense into yourself as you start to change your opinion of your body and yourself. For example, this book will teach you lots of way to incorporate new, healthy habits into your day to day: everything from knowing which foods to choose in a restaurant, to making some much needed "Me Time" for yourself to do anything from exercise to take a nap. I will teach you to treat yourself with so much loving care that it will be nearly impossible for you to wind up eating six consecutive slices of pizza and drinking a bottle and a half of Chardonnay in your pajamas. You will feel like such a goddess that the thought of eating cheap, greasy food will actually make you nauseous. But it's going to take work, and a lot of practice to get there.

So how is it done? Whenever you feel a moment of crazy coming on, I want you to stop and ask yourself these questions: Am I going to die? Is someone else going to die? Will the world end?

No matter what the situation, asking yourself these three questions is a surefire way to snap yourself back into reality rather quickly. Some instances where any of those questions will come in handy: when you get on the scale after a night out and you're up two pounds; when you see a photo of yourself at a wedding where you appear to have three chins; when your boyfriend says he's "not in the mood" and you immediately assume it's because he spotted that patch of cellulite on the back of your thigh. Truth is that none of that crap really matters. We get so caught up in obsessing over trivial things, especially when it comes to our weight. So lighten up and just picture the four-inch version of me with sparkly sound effects whenever you feel like you're about to board the train to crazy town.

Comparison Will Kill You

Can we just address this right now before we go any further? The fastest way to be miserable is to compare yourself – especially your body – to anyone else's. I can't even begin to tell you how many times I've stared obsessively for hours at photos of other women, trying to identify with someone who looked most like me, and then convince myself that she wasn't really "that fat." What a serious waste of time.

The fastest way to be miserable is to compare yourself – especially your body – to anyone else's.

I've seen countless women do this to themselves and guess what? It makes you even fatter. Yes, seriously. The more you stress and obsess, the more you self-sabotage and overeat. If you are that down on yourself, you're so much less likely to eat a super healthy dinner or go for a run on a Saturday morning. Instead, you'll be wasting that energy wishing you had your sister-in-law's ass. And that is a one-way track to Loserville.

Remember this: nobody in this world will have the exact same story as you, or the exact same body as you. Nobody in this world will lose weight at the exact same pace you do, or see results from working out the exact same way you do. You know that cute little Dr. Seuss quote, "There is no one alive who is Youer than You." We brainwash kids with that message because it's fucking true. So why can't you believe it? The sooner you realize that your body is a unique gem that is like no other, the quicker you'll be on your way to health and happiness. And the quicker you set goals that make sense for you and only you, the quicker you'll reach them. There is no "one size fits all" for weight, body type, or beauty. We don't all need to be a size two. Define your "happy place" when it comes to weight and health and do whatever it takes to get and stay there.

Define your "happy place" when it comes to weight
and health and do whatever it takes to get and stay there.

What Are You Waiting For?

A major theme of *The Champagne Diet* is "living your most effervescent life." Not ten pounds from now. Not next year when you're finally wearing a size eight. *Right now.* If I think back to all of the times in my life where I waited to do something until I lost weight, I get really sad. I missed out on so much: so many dips in the pool, trips to the beach, parties that I skipped out on because I didn't want to wear a sleeveless dress in the summer, dates I declined, and events that I didn't host because I felt like I wasn't thin enough yet. It really sickens me to think that I could have had so much more fun if I had just learned to let go a little and stop waiting to get skinny.

As women, we seem to have this idea that life will be perfect when we lose weight. We'll finally start that business, have the confidence to wear a bikini, or go on that vacation. We'll start dating when we're thin, and we'll be ballsy enough to ask for that promotion. It's completely ridiculous to assume that any of those things will be made possible by a shift of the scale. Guess what? It's the exact opposite. Once we start actually doing those things, the weight *will* come off. I promise you that. When you're fulfilled in your life, it is so much easier to eat healthier and eat less because you have so many exciting things going on. Think about that one for a moment.

Make a list of 3 things you're waiting to do until you lose weight:

1. _____
2. _____
3. _____

I want you to examine that list and come up with a valid reason for each one explaining why you need to be thin to do any of them. Remember, I said *valid*. Write the reasons below:

1. _____
2. _____
3. _____

If you actually filled anything out above, cross it out right now. It's bullshit and I don't buy it. There is nothing in this world that you should be waiting to do until you lose weight. Nothing! If that's your excuse, you're missing out on more than you can imagine. By the end of this book, I want you to promise me that you will have an action plan in place to do at least two of the things on that list. You don't have to have completed them, but you've got to at the very least be planning for them. Got it?

Now go and pour yourself a glass of champagne and get ready for the next chapter, which is sure to blow your pretty little mind and change the way you eat – forever.

Champagne Diet Manifesto

I truly believe I am worthy of an amazing life.
My weight does not define what I am
capable of or what I deserve.

CHAPTER TWO
The Big Fat Diet Business

I have tried nearly every single diet known to man. And none of them have worked (at least not in the long run). Images of overweight middle-aged women who have posters of cats with inspirational quotes on the walls of their Jenny Craig "personal coaching" offices scorch my brain, and I can recite the point value of nearly any edible food item on the planet – even some inedible things. Weight Watcher "Twinkies" anyone? Two points a pop, for the record.

My experience as a professional dieter dates back to my childhood. Picture it: Brooklyn, 1991. An eleven-year-old girl in an oversized Donny Wahlberg t-shirt and tangerine culottes is about to step on the scale. She'll lose a pound or two, and then head into a room full of adults, far more desperate and jaded than her, who will talk for an hour about how they skipped desert at a wedding that weekend, or how they had a fat-free muffin instead of their usual bacon egg and cheese for breakfast that day. While the room erupts in a round of applause, she'll survey the crowd and wonder why they all still kind of look fat, and even a little grey. She'll then go home and drink three cans of Diet Coke and tick off boxes in a paper journal, recording her meals for the day.

That eleven-year-old girl was me. And that scene was the beginning of a twenty-year journey of weight struggles, disordered eating, and body image issues that would consume me. Consume me so much, that it wasn't until I was nearly thirty before I got a handle on things and began to truly understand why my weight played such a huge role in my life and just what it would take to fix it. Luckily, I did come to understand why I battled with the bulge for much of my childhood and early adulthood, but it a long took time, many yo-yo diets, and lots of self-discovery. I was never fat – just always kind of chubby – which was almost worse, in my eyes.

You see, I never carried *that* much extra weight. No, instead, I was tortured by an extra fifteen-to-twenty pounds that seemed to stick to me like glue, regardless of my efforts. Even if they did disappear, it was short-lived. It was almost as if they mocked me, sometimes having a significant impact on my life – like during summers when my friends would carelessly frolic in bikinis and I'd hide under a sundress pretending I was worried about getting a sun burn. Other times, it didn't bother me much, like in the winter when I'd drape myself in the fabrics of denial, most often in the form of a cable knit sweater or loose-fitting cardigan. Seriously, thank God for seasons.

It was not until my late 20's that I finally saw with crystal clear vision I never truly learned how to eat healthy. Once I realized that it was not okay to eat diet cookies and chug Crystal Light all day (oops!), it was almost as if a light bulb went off in my head. *You mean drinking Diet Pepsi isn't just like drinking water? But Weight Watchers told me it was!* And no, I am not making that up; they actually did tell us that.

Four out of your eight recommended daily glasses of "water" could be consumed in the form of diet soda, at least in the 90s. And what's the big deal with drinking diet soda anyway, you may be wondering? Well, here are a few of the ingredients: Carbonated Water, Caramel Color, Aspertame, Phosphoric Acid, Potassium Benzoate, Caffeine, Citric Acid, Natural Flavor, Acesulfame

Potassium, Phenylalanine.

Does that sound anything like water to you? Me neither.

There are a slew of other dieting misconceptions that had become so ingrained in me, and so many of us, it's almost scary. We were taught that low-calorie was the way to go, no matter how processed or how laden with chemicals our foods were. As long as it was labeled "Zero" or "Light," it was for the taking.

Arriving at my good health epiphany was no easy road. It was littered with unhealthy relationships, complete and total meltdowns, and love affairs with powdered donuts (I mean, how delicious are they?), as well as an honesty with myself that I never had before. I finally came to realize that eating good food made me feel good, and *that* became the measure of my success. Not a number on the scale, not the size of my jeans. Once my emotions became my weight-loss barometer, I was suddenly free from a vicious cycle of dieting that plagued most of my life.

Once my emotions became my weight-loss barometer, I was suddenly free from a vicious cycle of dieting that plagued most of my life.

But that was only the first part of the battle. Eating healthy was great, but it did not make me skinny. Unfortunately, I didn't trade in Baked Doritos for bananas and suddenly get abs of steel. But I did work extremely hard at a little thing called self-compassion, which opened me up to a world of endless happiness, passion, and creativity. Being gentle with myself and being okay with the fact that I'd never be stick-thin was liberating. I learned to embrace my body – every last inch of it. Was I perfect? No. But who the hell is? My focus slowly shifted to other things besides my weight. I got to really know myself at the core: what I loved, what inspired me, and who I was outside of that number on the scale.

My personal experiences and understanding led me to become a life and wellness coach. After taking control of my life, I felt compelled to help other women do the same. I suddenly felt like I was let in on this huge secret and I had to share it with women everywhere. It kills me to see women suffer through this because I know exactly what it's like to have your weight control every single part of your life. It's torture. My clients are shocked when our sessions have hardly anything to do with food, and everything to do with what's going on in their pretty little heads. Until we get to the bottom of our emotional wellbeing, we will never be able to develop a positive relationship with our bodies. And if we never develop that relationship, we'll never be able to treat it the way we should.

How *The Champagne Diet* was Born

So, how exactly did *The Champagne Diet* come about? After years of losing and gaining weight, I found myself at a point where I was fed up. One day at work, while venting my frustrations about how I couldn't possibly eat another frozen diet burrito for dinner, my coworker's ears perked up. Liron, a drop-dead gorgeous former Israeli soldier who didn't take crap from anyone immediately barked back at me. "When are you gonna listen to me? You need to stop dieting. Just eat healthy!" she commanded.

I paused for a minute, both confused and intrigued. Liron had the sexiest and scariest accent you could ever imagine – the kind of voice that you just had to listen to, no matter what she was saying. Curious, I asked her to continue. "What do you mean by healthy?"

"You know, cut the shit!"

Those three simple words struck a chord with me. *Cut the shit*. It sounded so easy coming from someone else. Liron went on to instruct me on the "good" foods and "bad" foods I should be having daily: whole grains, lean proteins, and fresh fruits and vegetables were on top of the list. Anything with preservatives or crazy ingredients I couldn't pronounce was forbidden. Easy peasy. But I had one burning question.

"Can I still drink?" I asked her.

"Yes. Just drink champagne," she yelled back at me.

Hello? Champagne? My eyeballs lit up like a Christmas tree. "What? How? Why?" I stuttered.

My Champagne Solider went on to explain that a glass of sparkling wine only has about 90 calories, making it one of the lightest drinks out there. And come on; is it not so incredibly sexy to sip on a glass of bubbly? Immediately I was sold. And *The Champagne Diet* was born.

As part of my new bubbly makeover, Liron also taught me to "cut the shit" from my life, as well. Her fierce attitude rubbed off on me, and as I lost weight, I also lost a few bad habits – including an unhealthy relationship that I had spent the better part of my 20's in with someone who constantly made me feel like my weight was a determining factor in his feelings toward me.

Outside of eating and drinking well, I introduced a few rituals of my own to this new lifestyle including choosing something to toast to every time I drank champagne. Whether I was lounging on my couch after a long day of work, or out celebrating with friends, I always raise my glass and celebrate something, no matter how big or small. With my newly detoxed body and life, I went on to lose weight, and gain an unstoppable sense of confidence. I was happier and healthier than ever.

Outside of eating and drinking well, I introduced a few rituals of my own to this new lifestyle including choosing something to toast to every time I drank champagne. Whether I was lounging on my couch after a long day of work, or out celebrating with friends, I always raise my glass and celebrate something, no matter how big or small.

Owning Your Health

Since creating and adopting *The Champagne Diet* as my way of life for the past six years, I have spent an incredible amount time learning about health and wellness. I'm horrified to remember what I was putting in my body for years—the chemicals and preservatives that did nothing to help me either lose weight or get healthy. What's even more upsetting is the fact that diet companies are cashing in on our ignorance.

Americans spend $40 billion a year on weight-loss programs and products. $40 billion! Companies promising quick results and "guaranteed success" are laughing all the way to the bank as people keep joining, and re-joining their programs time and time again. No matter what poison you pick, there is a very slim chance you'll stay on any diet plan for the rest of your life. And because diet plans aren't sustainable, you'll most likely gain back the weight you lost, and come running back for more. It's a sick cycle that does nothing for us, but continually makes us feel like failures.

So why are we such suckers? What's with the hold these companies seem to have on us? I'll tell you: they sell hope to desperate people. Desperate people like you and me, convinced by society that we should look like Nicole Richie in her ribs-a-plenty bikini photo shoot. These corporations know we are dying (sometimes literally) to lose weight. They play on our insecurities. And frankly, I am over it. Think about it: do you want to keep falling victim to this trap? I sure don't.

On nearly every diet plan out there, points values and calorie counting trump balanced, whole foods. Sure, they may suggest eating a certain portion of vegetables or fruits daily, but look at any diet company who packages and sells their own food, and flip the box over. Once you're done reading the myriad of chemical ingredients in their "meals," get back to me. The calories and fat content may be low, and maybe even there's a ton of fiber and protein. Woohoo! But what about what's actually *in it*? You'll be shocked to learn just how much toxic garbage we are consuming under the guise of "healthy."

Take for example, a seemingly harmless *Weight Watchers Smart Ones Pepperoni Pizza*. This used to be an all-time favorite of mine. It only "cost me" six points, and it took less than five minutes to make. The perfect complement to a long day at work, right? Wrong! Behold the ingredients list: Stone-Fired Pizza Crust (Wheat Flour, Water, Yeast, Sugar, Garlic Powder, Onion Powder, Olive Oil, Baking Powder [Sodium Acid Pyrophosphate, Bicarbonate Soda, Corn Starch, Monocalcium Phosphate], Salt), Sauce (Tomato Puree [Tomato Paste, Water], Water, Seasoning [Corn Maltodextrin, Sugar, Spices, Garlic, Onion, Xanthan Gum, Citric Acid, Dextrose, Acetic Acid, Natural Flavor, Extractives of Paprika], Modified Cornstarch, Salt, Garlic Powder), Reduced Fat/Reduced Sodium Mozzarella Cheese (Part Skim Milk, Nonfat Milk, Modified Cornstarch, Cheese Culture, Salt, Potassium Chloride, Flavors, Annatto, Vitamin A Palmitate, Enzymes), Pepperoni (Pork, Beef, Salt, Spices, Dextrose, Seasoning [Spice Extractives, Paprika Oleoresin, Smoke Flavoring, BHA, BHT, Citric Acid], Lactic Acid Starter Culture, Sodium Nitrite), Parmesan Cheese (Part-Skim Cows

Milk, CheeseCultures, Salt, Enzymes), Romano Cheese (Part Skim Cow's Milk, Cheese Culture,Salt, Enzymes), Parsley.

I'm sorry, but what the fuck?

On *The Champagne Diet*, we eat clean, glamorous meals that look pretty on our plates and nourish our bodies, and I'll teach you how to do that in the next chapter. If we don't recognize the ingredients, we don't eat them – at least not very often (remember, we're not into deprivation here).

And don't even get me started on the sodium content of "diet" foods. I never paid attention to sodium or the way it affected me until I started to actually eat real food. I noticed that my entire face changed when I was eating meals that didn't have 1,000 mg of sodium per pop. Eating fresh food that is lightly salted is a whole other ballgame than eating prepared meals that are loaded with sodium. Ever wonder why you feel so damn bloated sometimes? Why you can actually weigh five pounds more on the scale in the morning after a night of eating garbage? Blame it on the sodium, baby.

Now, don't get me wrong here – you do need some method to monitor your calorie intake, especially when losing weight. It would be impossible to guess the amount of food you should be eating in a day, especially when you're so used to overeating. My one exception to the "diets suck" rule is Weight Watchers for the point counting method only. Based on their point system, they factor in the fat, carbs, fiber, and protein in food. I never had long-term success with Weight Watchers in the past because I lived off their frozen chemical bombs that did absolutely nothing for my health except probably help rot some of my insides. But when I began using the program strictly for portion control and actually started cooking and preparing my own meals after I gained the "Newlywed Twenty," it did help me lose the weight. You see, I'm a pro at maintaining my weight, but I sometimes need to reel it in when it comes to losing, and I can't always do it alone. I didn't eat any Weight Watchers "food" this time. I followed my *Champagne Diet* style of eating: whole, nutritious, real foods, and didn't give up my wine or champagne. I just ate and drank less of it all. If I had continued eating seven point Santa Fe Chicken frozen dinners, I'd be unsatisfied, unhealthy and probably still fat.

My Problem with "Cheat Days"

What if I told you not to think of the color green for the next thirty minutes? Whatever you do, don't think about the color green. If you do, bad things will happen. Every five minutes, I will remind you not to think about green. Guess what will happen? The color green will probably be the only thing you'll be able to think about.

One of the biggest problems with diets is the obsessive focus about what we should and should not be eating, and when we should and should not be eating it. On *The Champagne Diet*, there are no "cheat days." I don't starve all week so that I can go buckwild on an enormous plate of lasagna and an entire bread basket on a Saturday night. So many traditional diets teach us to reserve one day a week to splurge, so long as we're "good" all the other days. You hear celebrities talking about it all the time. "I eat a macrobiotic diet all week long and then on the weekends I allow myself to indulge in as much chocolate cake as I want!" This is one of the most self-destructive things we can do. Because by the time you reach that cheat day, you're so fucking starving that you dive head first into whatever it is you've been fantasizing about all week long. And you don't just eat it like a normal person. You *go to town*. You're so friggin' excited that you're "allowed" to eat that meal that you eat to the point where you are overfull, and then you wind up feeling guilty and gross.

If we just allowed ourselves to indulge in what we want with no restrictions, we'd eat a whole lot less. If you gave yourself permission to get a slice of pizza any night of the week, you'd loosen the rules around eating well and losing weight, which would immediately take a ton of stress off your shoulders. And you'd probably eat pizza a lot less often when it's not such a novelty.

Also, I'm kind of into living life. A world without pasta and wine is a pretty sad world in my eyes. I would personally rather be ten pounds heavier and actually look forward to meals, rather than be a starving, miserable twig. I love going out to fabulous dinners and indulging in delicious, real food. I love trying new wines. I love *experiencing life*. The problem is that diet companies brainwash us into thinking that life has to stop in order to lose weight. They tell us it's healthier to eat a 200-calorie frozen version of Tortellini Alfredo than it is to just eat the real fucking thing, even if the 200-calorie version is made up entirely of chemicals. We've become so convinced that real food is bad for us, and we've got to break the cycle.

A world without pasta and wine is a pretty sad
world in my eyes. I would personally rather be ten pounds
heavier and actually look forward to meals, rather
than be a starving, miserable twig.

Nothing Tastes as Good as Being Healthy Feels

Do you remember that quote from Kate Moss a few years back? She famously said, "Nothing tastes as good as being skinny feels." I remember women everywhere quoting her, feeling like they had some sort of epiphany after hearing those eight words. It was plastered across magazines as inspiration for women to lose weight. And I've seen women use that motto as a way to manipulate themselves into skipping meals, as I'm sure Kate did, too.

I understand what Miss Moss was getting at. She was trying to live by a mantra that kept her focused on her main goal, which was being skinny. Let's flip it a bit: what if we said, "Nothing tastes as good as being healthy feels." Doesn't that sound so much better? It works, too. Thinking about what you're putting in your body and how it will benefit your health shifts your perspective. Whenever I've had the urge to make a shitty choice, I ask myself, "What will this do for my body?" For example, a plate of fried onion rings probably won't do much other than upset my stomach. So maybe instead I want to snack on some raw bell peppers dipped in hummus. The hummus is full of protein, and the peppers have potassium, as well as vitamins A, B, C, and E. When you break it down like that, it's easy to make the better choice.

Sadly, most of these commercial diet programs will never educate us to think this way. They will continue to shove synthetic, fat-free cheese down our throats and tell us we can eat as much of it as we want as long as it fits in our calorie bank. They will never take responsibility for our health and the emotional reasons behind why we eat the way they should. They'll just keep on selling the dream. So we need to take responsibility for our own health and well-being, ladies. Whether you're on a mission to lose or maintain your weight, you need to do it in the healthiest way possible if you want to revamp your lifestyle and keep it off. Every single thing we put in our mouths is a choice. Let's start owning it.

Champagne Diet Manifesto

I take responsibility for my own health.
I focus on health over weight-loss and accept
that there is no "quick fix."

CHAPTER THREE

Beautiful Foods:
How and Why You Should Glamorize Your Meals

On *The Champagne Diet*, there are a few rules to abide by, and one of them is this: glamorize your meals. What does that mean? Well, it's two-fold. By glamorizing your meals, I mean you should be eating whole, nutritious, healthy foods only. Gorgeous plates awash with fresh vegetables, fruit, whole grains, and lean, clean protein. Think about beautiful foods that will nourish and energize you – as opposed to fatty, fake, disgusting foods that will leave you bloated and tired. You should either completely eliminate or strongly limit your intake of anything processed. Processed food is filled with chemicals and preservatives and it usually comes in a box or a bag and it's just downright *gross*.

Secondly, be conscious of *how* you eat. For example, avoid shoving a slice of pizza down your throat while you're Facebook stalking your ex-boyfriend in your pajamas. Instead, wrap yourself in your favorite silk robe and enjoy a delicate piece of salmon with sautéed asparagus and a glass of champagne. Make sure you're fully focused on your meal. Take breaths between each bite, and savor your food. And an added bonus: studies show that people who take time to fully chew their food actually digest their food better than those who eat quickly.

Avoid shoving a slice of pizza down your throat
while Facebook stalking your ex-boyfriend in your pajamas.
Instead, wrap yourself in your favorite silk robe and
enjoy a delicate piece of salmon with sautéed
asparagus and a glass of champagne.

The most important thing to realize though is that we're all going to have days where we inhale that slice of pizza. And that's okay! Don't beat yourself up. *The Champagne Diet* is not about punishment or negative self-talk. It's about self-compassion and forgiveness. If you had a David Hasselhoff moment and found yourself drunk on the kitchen floor with a cheeseburger at 3 am, just pick yourself up by the stilettos and get back on track tomorrow.

How to Glamorize Your Meals

I've seen it happen countless times: women approach me who want to get healthy and start taking care of themselves, but they have no idea where to begin. And that is completely fine. I am a firm believer in baby steps. In fact, I think baby steps are brilliant. When we bite off more than we can chew, (no pun intended), we often crash and burn. So let's start with the basics: what's in your refrigerator right now? I want you to take stock of everything on your shelves, your pantry, and your secret stash – all of it. Write down everything that's "questionable" and set it aside. You may already know that diet soda is like drinking poison, and if you don't, I'm telling you right now. So pour that shit down the drain. Maybe you're unsure about those diet cookies? Ditch them also. Here's something to keep in mind: anything that has the word "diet" in it is off limits. Trash it all, baby.

If you're wondering what you should be eating and drinking now that your cupboards are bare, have no fear. There are plenty of delicious, healthy options out there, and I'm going to give you some really great basics to get you started so that you can begin glamorizing your meals, *Champagne Diet* style.

Let's begin with grocery shopping. Your supermarket experience should mainly take place around the perimeter of the store. That means shopping in the aisles where the food and products are perishable, with a heavy focus on fresh, organic produce. *The Champagne Diet* is not limited to a vegetarian or vegan diet, however if you do choose to eat meat or eggs, you should make sure that what you are eating is antibiotic-free, hormone-free, grass-fed, etc. I'm not going to sit here and preach to you about animal cruelty, you can research that on your own time, and you should. It's a personal choice whether or not you want to eat animal products, but if you do, please be aware of where your food is coming from. All meat is not created equal.

If you're single, or think there's not a shot in hell you can convince your partner to go along for this ride (yet), don't worry. I know how hard it is to keep fresh produce, especially if you're the only one eating it. As an alternative to fresh veggies, bags of organic vegetables that are frozen at their peak of freshness are fantastic for you. Rule of thumb: always flip the bag over and make sure no other ingredients are listed other than the vegetable itself. Creamed spinach and broccoli in cheese sauce is a no-no. Stick with strictly organic veggies you can trust.

Go Organic

Why go organic? There are plenty of reasons. Is it more expensive? It can be, but when you learn why it's so much better for you, the choice should be pretty clear, and worth every penny. The word "organic" refers to the way farmers grow and process food like fruits, vegetables, grains, dairy products and meat. Organic farming practices are different than conventional farming. In organic farming, the goal is to encourage soil and water conservation and reduce pollution. Another difference is that organic farmers don't use chemicals to kill weeds. Instead, they'll use methods like sophisticated crop rotations to keep weeds at bay.

Some other benefits of eating organic are in the way plants are fertilized. Organic farmers will use natural fertilizers to promote plant growth as opposed to the chemical fertilizers conventional farmers use. Organic farmers also use natural insecticides to avoid pests and rodents. Conventional farmers use synthetic pesticides that can be harmful to us when ingested. They are spraying this stuff directly on the foods we eat. Do you want that in your body? I sure don't. Poison is *not* glamorous.

It's also important to know how to read labels when you shop. It can be intimidating to shop for good foods, so being aware of what labels represent is crucial. When food is labeled "100% Organic" it means exactly that − the food must be all organic or made of all organic ingredients. If something is just labeled "Organic" it means that at least 95 percent of the ingredients are organic. And be super careful of foods labeled "Natural" − this does not imply it is 100% organic, or even partially organic, and companies often use that label to deceive customers. Be thorough, do your research, and know what you're buying.

Another thing I should point out: eating glamorously and healthfully doesn't have to break the bank. To save cash, eat in season. Fruit and vegetables that are abundant will always be cheaper, even the organic ones. Try to hit up your local farmer's markets for locally grown produce; it's always guaranteed to cost less because it doesn't travel far. And for the things you do need to splurge on, know that your health is the best investment you can make. Don't go crying that fresh, wild salmon is too expensive when you're walking around with an iPhone. I won't buy that for a second! Cut out the crap from your life so you can afford to eat the way you should. It's all about priorities, and investing in yourself and your health is the best choice you will ever make.

My Case for Plant-Based

As I've said earlier, *The Champagne Diet* is not a diet, so I won't tell you that you should or should not eat meat. That's on you. I personally follow a vegetarian diet (and sometimes moonlight as a vegan), because that works for me. And pssst! Sometimes I even eat meat if I'm craving it. It's not often, but it happens, and I don't beat myself up over it. You've gotta listen to your body and do what works for you. But I will say this: a plant-based (or vegan diet – they're the same thing) when done right never hurt anyone. In fact, studies have proven that a plant-based diet can actually reverse disease and is one of the healthiest ways you can eat.

So what exactly does all this vegan, plant-based stuff mean? It calls for eating foods with absolutely no animal products: no dairy, no meat, and no fish – none of it. To truly eat plant-based, you should be eating mainly fresh fruits, vegetables, legumes, and whole grains. But beware: Oreos are considered vegan (now don't get any ideas, okay?). You want to make sure that you're focusing on a balanced, nutritious diet void of junk if you're going the plant-based route. I followed a plant-based diet for two months before writing this book, and although I felt great, I found that it just wasn't sustainable for my lifestyle. I work a lot, and found it was difficult to be limited to meals that I mostly had to cook. Unless you're grabbing lunch on the go at a vegan restaurant, animal products are in almost *everything*.

A plant-based diet never hurt anyone. In fact, studies have proven that a plant-based diet can actually reverse disease and is one of the healthiest ways you can eat.

As wonderful as it is to eat vegan, don't think you need to be all or nothing. One of my clients eats one vegan meal per day, and I love that. It's her way of being health conscious in a way that works for her lifestyle.

Even the New York Times' famous food writer Mark Bittman is "vegan before 6 PM," meaning he follows a vegan diet all day and then eats what he wants for dinner. In his book *VB6: Eat Vegan Before 6:00 to Lose Weight and Restore Your Health … for Good* he talks about how easy it is to follow that lifestyle, and how anyone can do it. The suggestion to go vegan actually came from Bittman's doctor after a check-up revealed he was forty pounds overweight, his cholesterol was fifty points higher than it should be, and his blood sugar was high. Because he writes about food for a living, he couldn't become 100% vegan, and he didn't even want to. His doctor told him to get creative, and he did. By following a vegan diet until 6 PM, he's able to get healthier but also indulge in all the foods he loves during dinner-time. It was a happy medium and a compromise that he could live with.

And the results were fantastic. He lost weight and felt better than ever. Bittman admits he "cheats" whenever he wants and doesn't pressure himself to stick to a rigid vegan diet during the day. For example, he'll throw a splash of half-and-half in his coffee when he craves it, or grab a slice of pizza for lunch with his co-workers at the office.

I love Mark Bittman's approach, and I find myself eating in a very similar way. I now follow a vegetarian diet, but like I said, I still incorporate a lot of my vegan ways into my eating habits. For instance, green juice is my religion. If I go a day without it, I can tell a difference in the way I feel physically and mentally. I suck these babies down each morning, and opt for juices packed with spinach, kale, apple, cucumber and lemon. Sometimes I vary the blend, but kale and spinach are always the star of the show. They are so full of nutrients that it's almost impossible not to feel amazing after drinking one. Green juice is truly a part of my *Champagne Diet*. In fact, sometimes I even drink mine in a flute. Glamour baby, glamour!

So what if you're not at the point where you can drink your veggies? That's totally fine. Start by incorporating dark, leafy greens into your every day – in any form. Whether you're drinking them, cooking them, or eating them raw, greens are wonderful for you. Both spinach and kale are chock full of vitamins A, C and K, along with folic acid, magnesium, and potassium. Kale also contains carotenoids, including beta-carotene, which are antioxidants with natural anti-inflammatory properties that may help prevent some forms of cancer. And if you could care less about vitamins, then know this: greens make your skin glow. I'm talking full on, shimmering, gorgeous skin. These veggies are so nourishing and hydrating; you'll never need another BB cream again.

The most important thing to remember is that any change is a good change. You don't have to be completely reformed to shift your health for the better. Baby steps are key, and remember to be gentle on yourself. If you try to go vegetarian and decide to eat a steak one night, the world will not end and you will not die (remember our ass-kicking questions from Chapter One!). Always remember to celebrate all of the positive healthy choices you've been making and don't harp on the bad ones. We're all human and improving your lifestyle is a process.

Make a list of three ways you can add glamour to your meals:

1. _____
2. _____
3. _____

Get Real

Something I really want to stress is this: perfection is a myth. There is no way you're going to eat perfectly and healthfully at all times. What I want you to do is aim for improvement. Make the best choices possible as often as you can. I'd be lying to you and myself if I said I ate 100% organic non-processed foods at all times. It's just impossible and it sets the stage for feelings of failure if you convince yourself you can do that. Do I still sometimes put flavored coffee in my creamer? Yes. Do I sometimes rip off a hunk of Italian bread and eat it? Hell, yeah, I do. But I don't do it every day. And that's what counts.

I remember when I was following a vegan diet, I judged myself a lot. And to be quite candid, that's a big reason why I gave it up. I became so obsessive about not eating animal products to the point where I'd send food back in a restaurant if I thought my rice had been cooked in chicken broth or there was a hint of cheese in a sauce. When I craved a piece of cheese, I felt like I was failing somehow, and if I gave in it would mean I wasn't good enough. It was almost as if I was in some sort of competition with myself to see how long I could hold out. Although I was eating supremely well, there was ultimately nothing healthy about it.

When I decided to go from a vegan diet to a vegetarian one, everything changed for me. I was happier and it felt like something I could live with. I chose vegetarian mainly because I truly don't like eating meat, and I had previously been a vegetarian for years. Meat has never been something I've craved, and to be honest it just sort of freaks me out. So the choice was natural and doable. I didn't judge or obsess. I just ate in a way that made sense for my lifestyle. And like I said earlier, if I want a giant piece of steak one day, I'm going to eat it.

So as you move through this book, please remember to take my advice in a way that works for you. If you can't part with Splenda just yet, don't freak out. Make other healthier choices like incorporating more fruits and veggies into your day. Start with what feels right to you, and tackle the harder obstacles later. If you're a diet soda maniac, it might be frustrating to try and quit cold turkey. So start small. Reduce your intake from four cans a day to one. Be real with yourself and remember that any improvement is good.

Stop Bitching and Get in the Kitchen

None of this is going to be a walk in the park. In order to live a healthy life, you're going to have to put some work into it, and that's where a lot of people fail. But have no fear: I am here to give you all the short-cuts and teach you how to make it fun and doable. You're gonna have to get in that kitchen and become friendly with your oven. Now, before you panic, realize that I'm not telling you that you need to master every single one of Julia Child's recipes, but if you hop on over to Pinterest or any of the websites I'm going to mention below, I can promise you that you'll find healthy, easy recipes that will nourish your body and taste delicious. Here are a few of my favorites:

Skinnytaste.com – This site is amazing. It's chock-full of recipes that are categorized by point value, if you're interested in portion control. The founder, Gina, has been running the site since 2008 so the archives are rich and thorough.

Eat-Yourself-Skinny.com – I adore this site! The founder, Kelly Hunt, is one of the sweetest people ever and she's so inspiring and motivational. Her recipes rock and her photos make you want to jump through the computer screen and immediately eat whatever she's posting. She also posts lots of workout motivation on her Instagram account, which is an added plus.

Pinterest.com – If you go on Pinterest and type "healthy recipes" in the search box, you will get a slew of amazing options. The great thing about Pinterest is that you can click on the image and it will take you right to the original site that the recipe came from. You can search by vegetarian, organic, vegan, whatever floats your nutritional boat.

I used to dread cooking. I felt like I had to buy 900 ingredients and spend tons of money to make the perfect meal. But that sentiment could not be further from the truth. Do you know how easy it is to buy a bunch of fresh veggies and throw them in a wok with a little spicy Asian sauce? (I'm referring to the all-natural ones that are low in sodium— I'm not talking about drenching them in General Tso's sauce here). Get yourself to a Whole Foods or some type of market like it and stock up on those microwavable organic brown rice cups. They sell ones that aren't laden with chemicals and they literally take 90 seconds to heat up. Pair that with your spicy Asian veggies and you've got yourself a meal.

Or one of my favorite things to do is go pick up a piece of freshly prepared fish from my favorite local restaurant. I dread preparing fish on my own. It's just a major pain in the ass for me, and I'm the only one in my house who eats it, so I let the restaurant do the work there. I order whatever fish I'm having (salmon, halibut, shrimp) without sides and prepare my own at home. For example, a local bistro in my neighborhood makes *the best* salmon. They prepare fresh, wild salmon in a white wine sauce with lemon and capers. Could I make that myself? Sure, but who's got time for that? And why would I compete with the best? I love the way they make it, so before dinner, I pick up the fish from the restaurant, then I go home and sauté some fresh spinach as a side and voila. Dinner is served.

So ladies, please don't be afraid to cook. It truly is the key to healthy eating, and you'd be surprised at how fun and easy it can be. Start small and experiment with a few dishes. And don't forget to wear a cute little apron, put on some lipstick, and sip on a glass of wine while you're cooking. Make it an experience that you enjoy and look forward to.

Champagne Diet Rituals

Aside from consuming unprocessed, nutrient-rich foods, there are some other healthy habits that every *Champagne Dieter* should explore. Creating rituals that support a healthy mind and body are crucial to our well-being. If our mind and bodies are not in sync, nothing will function as it should. And for busy women, this is especially important.

One of my favorite rituals is drinking water with fresh lemon. Bonus points if you put it in a fancy wine glass! The benefits of drinking lemon water are endless. For starters, lemons are an excellent source of Vitamin C, which helps boost our immune systems. Lemons also help balance our pH levels, which can help us avoid disease. By balancing our pH, our bodies function in an alkaline state, which puts everything in check, promoting weight loss and digestion. Lemon water is also super hydrating and energizing. Do you see what a little twist can do for ya? Try to add lemon water to your daily routine – either in the morning, or at night, or both.

Creating rituals that support a healthy mind and body
are crucial to our well-being. If our mind and bodies are not in
sync, nothing will function as it should.

Another fabulous ritual I've come to love is drinking tea. It's no secret that I adore my wine and champagne – in fact at one point, Happy Hour was becoming a nightly ritual for me, and for all the wrong reasons. I found myself craving wine at night to escape from my day – not because I wanted to enjoy a glass with dinner. Before I knew it, one glass became two, and two became three, and I found myself over-indulging on a nightly basis. As a result, I snacked more and my sleep was disrupted. Not to mention, I was packing on a few extra hundred calories *every single day*!

I had to find a healthy alternative for at least a few weeknights when I needed to be as well-rested as possible. I knew wine represented relaxation and peace to me, so I was tasked with finding a new ritual that would give me the same feeling. Enter tea. I quickly became hooked on Yogi Tea, specifically, because of the inspirational messages on each tea bag. If you've never tried it, go pick up a box tonight. You will become *obsessed*. Each tea serves a different purpose: some energize, some calm the mind, some aid in healthy detoxification, while others ease tension. The flavors are amazing and the herbal blends provide tons of health benefits. I now indulge in my "tea time" on certain weeknights when I know I have a big day the next day, and I save my wine and champagne for weekends and nights when I can truly enjoy it – and usually by that point I'm salivating for a glass. It's nice to have something to look forward to after a long day.

Champagne Diet Manifesto

I indulge in delicious, whole foods that energize my body,
mind and soul. I create nourishing rituals to restore
balance and wellness in my life.

CHAPTER FOUR

There's Always Room For Champagne

By this point, you're probably thinking, okay, so where exactly *does* champagne fit in? We've covered the benefits of eating well, and now I'm going to fill you in on how to drink well, too. In this chapter, we'll talk all about indulging in our bubbles and why champagne (in moderation) is actually good for you! I'll also tell you why champagne is my go-to drink whether I'm relaxing by myself after a long day at work or hosting a fabulous dinner party. Whether you're reaping the cardiovascular benefits, increasing your sex drive, or just spicing up an ordinary Tuesday night, champagne is *magic*.

Let's start with the obvious: the calorie factor. Drinking can pack on pounds quickly if you're not careful. Mixed drinks are the absolute worst, carrying anywhere from 200-500 calories per drink, depending on what you order. Wine and beer come in at a close second, with around 150-200 calories a pop. But champagne, as I mentioned in the previous chapters, has just around 90 calories per flute. Now keep in mind, I'm talking about a five-ounce pour. If you're drinking your bubbly out of a fishbowl glass, you're going to wind up drinking a lot more calories than anticipated (and probably wind up with a massive hangover). But if you indulge in a glass or two, you'll enjoy a nice buzz all for under approximately 200 calories. Sound good? I think so, too!

But it's not just the calorie count that makes champagne so

appealing. Numerous studies continue to come out in support of champagne's health benefits and I've got the scoop for you.

Bubbles on the Brain:
How Champagne Can Improve Brain Function

According to Urban Dictionary, "Champagne Brain" is defined as "the crazy, severe hangover you get the morning after ballin' out of control and consuming copious amounts of champagne." While that is what can happen if you're drinking your face off in "da club" till 4 am, the "Champagne Brain" I'm going to talk about in this chapter is much healthier and much more beneficial to your overall well-being.

Research now shows that champagne, when consumed in moderation, can actually protect the brain against injuries that occur during stroke and other illnesses including Alzheimer's and Parkinson's. This is excellent news for those of us who want to remember our names and family members for as long as possible.

Studies now show that champagne, when consumed
in moderation, can actually protect the brain against injuries
that occur during stroke and other illnesses including
Alzheimer's and Parkinson's.

The Journal of Agricultural and Food Chemistry reports on the findings, which were a collaboration between researchers at the University of Reading in England and the Università degli studi di Cagliari, located in Monserrato, Italy. The study showed that drinking champagne responsibly may benefit one's health because previous research has shown the sparkling wine contains high amounts of polyphenols. If you're thinking, what the Hello Kitty are polyphenols, have no fear. I had no idea either. These glorious little antioxidants are found in wine and champagne, and prevent cell death from oxidative stress.

While the polyphenol count in red wine is greater than that in sparkling wine, champagne contains certain types of beneficial phenolic compounds including tyrosol and caffeic acid. According to researchers, these anti-inflammatory substances may help to regulate cells' response to injury while helping to clean up and remove dangerous chemicals from your body.

The polyphenols in sparkling wine are also able to cross the blood-brain barrier and may therefore confer benefits to the entire central nervous system. All that is wonderful, and if you don't understand it, it doesn't really matter. Just know that it means one thing: bring on the bubbly.

Another more recent study shows that three glasses of champagne a week can actually stave off Alzheimer's and Dementia. This research, also from Reading University, showed that a compound found in both Pinot noir and Pinot meunier, both of which are in champagne, can actually help boost our memory. The experiments were conducted on rats, which had champagne mashed into their food every day for six weeks (lucky little rats!). Each rat was then left to run in a maze to find a treat. Five minutes later, the exercise was repeated to see if the rat had remembered where it was found. Without champagne, the rats had a fifty percent success rate, but after a "glass" their score shot up to an average seventy percent. Researchers concluded that this was a dramatic improvement. Pretty amazing stuff, huh? It would be even more amazing if they actually gave the rats miniature champagne flutes, but my guess is no.

All of this research is absolutely fantastic, but please keep in mind, ladies, we don't want to overindulge, or we'll wind up with more health problems than we bargained for. And nobody looks cute when they're sloppy drunk or suffering from sclerosis of the liver. These studies show that champagne and sparkling wine help our brain when we're drinking bubbles in moderation – not when we're having it for breakfast.

Heart Smart:
How Champagne Can Improve Cardiovascular Health

Heart health. It is a hot topic in all the women's magazines. We're constantly getting inundated with articles that tell us red wine is good for our heart. But our good friend red has some competition in the heart attack prevention game. Her name is champagne (ooh la la!).

Leave it to the French and the Brits to come up with this one, and be thankful they did. According to a study published in the British Journal of Nutrition, conducted by researchers in both Reading, England with the help of scientists from Reims, France, people who consumed moderate amounts of champagne each day showed improved arterial function.

The researchers decided to do the study after realizing champagne had never really been evaluated as a source for heart health benefits. After learning about the benefits of red wine, they went ahead and tested the effects of bubbly on volunteers aged 25-60. During the test, some of the volunteers were asked to drink champagne, while the other drank a carbonated, fruity beverage. (I know which one I'd want to be).

After the volunteers chugged their respective cocktails, or mocktails, their blood was taken. It turned out that the champagne drinkers showed high levels of nitric oxide, a molecule that controls blood pressure. Optimal nitric oxide levels should decrease the risk of blood clots forming and, therefore, the study concludes, this should equally decrease the likelihood of heart disease and strokes.

So now we know that champagne can make you skinny, keep you from going crazy, and help you avoid a massive heart attack.

But there is one more benefit to bubbly that will have you filling your glass faster than you can say, "I'm horny." That's right kittens; champagne is a proven libido booster.

Bubbly in the Boudoir:
How Champagne Can Improve Your Sex Life

Aside from celebrations, champagne is synonymous with romance. Bubbly is always the star of the show on Valentine's Day, it's a main character in all Danielle Steel novels, and it's the perfect companion for those nights in the hot tub with your sweetie. And that is no coincidence. Research now shows that champagne is proven to increase sex drive. Go ahead, pinch yourself, ladies.

I don't know about you, but I've been searching for an excuse to keep a bottle of champagne on my nightstand. I can't think of anything more glamorous than sipping a glass in my favorite silk nightgown. Vodka and sex? So college. Beer and sex? Not unless you're doing it under the bleachers at a baseball game with a hot Yankee (not in *this* lifetime). So scratch all those drinks off your list. It's all about the bubbles in the bedroom!

So why is champagne so great for our sex lives? One reason for this wondrous little discovery has to do with the carbonation in champagne. The bubbles hit your bloodstream quicker, therefore giving you a warm, tingly feeling faster than any other type of alcohol. It's no wonder you're giggling yourself into oblivion after two sips of it. And who wouldn't want to crawl into bed with their honey after feeling like *that*? But ladies, beware. We don't want to give our man too much of the good stuff, or we'll wind up with a situation on our hands that is less than desirable, if you know what I mean.

The next discovery that attributes champagne as the reason for increased libido is the most fun, in my opinion. The late Dr. Max Lake, a vintner and MD in Australia, discovered that the scent of some types of champagne replicated the scent of certain female pheromones. Look for wines that have a heavy yeasty, brie cheese, bread-dough notes. Who needs Chanel No. 5? The trick to turning your man on lies right in the bottom of your flute. Bottoms up, girls!

Why Champagne Makes Everything Better

It's pretty obvious that I adore champagne. And now that you've learned about all of the wonderful benefits to drinking it, can you blame me? But my passion for bubbles goes far beyond all of those amazing things. There is just something so damn sexy about a glass of champagne. From its golden hue, to the tiny bubbles that seem to just dance in your glass, champagne is just divine.

One of the things I love most about champagne is the way it can spice up an ordinary moment and truly make it extraordinary. Whenever I'm going to a friend's house, I always bring a bottle of bubbly. And it doesn't have to be expensive, French champagne either. Picking up a $12 bottle of sparkling wine can elevate a regular girl's night in to a chic, fabulous, mini soiree. The moment that bottle is popped, something happens. The whole vibe changes. Suddenly, everyone is giddy. And don't tell me you don't feel so incredibly gorgeous holding a glass of champagne. It's an instant dose of glamour!

When I'm having guests over for dinner, champagne is always on hand. People usually expect white or red wine, but by opening a bottle of champagne in your home, you evoke a sense of allure and excitement. And let me tell you – your guests will be so impressed that they'll be asking when your next dinner party is before they've even eaten their appetizers.

I also love opening a bottle of champagne when I'm at home, either alone or with my hubby. It can take an average Tuesday evening and make it feel like a celebration. And when you pair a glass of champagne with your dinner, you are far less likely to overeat because the whole mood has shifted. You suddenly feel like a dazzlingly hot goddess, and who wants to pig out when you feel that good?

I also love opening a bottle of champagne when I'm at home, either alone or with my hubby. It can take an average Tuesday evening and make it feel like a celebration.

So the next time you're heading to a dinner party, or just heading home to make yourself dinner, pick up a bottle of bubbly on the way. And if you're not sure what to buy, go to a wine shop that you trust and ask the employees to give you some recommendations based on your taste preference and budget. You'd be surprised at how accessible and affordable sparkling wine is.

Healthy Hangover Cures

Let's be real here: if you're reading this book, you like your cocktails. You've probably over-indulged in the good stuff more than once, and you've probably stuffed yourself with greasy food the next morning to nurse your hangover. That cycle usually leads to feeling worse in more ways than one. You feel guilty for pigging out on that bacon egg and cheese sandwich (or whatever your fattening food of choice was), and you feel even worse physically because the grease does nothing to sooth your already upset stomach. The morning after a night of heavier-than-usual drinking, your poor body is racing to break down all of the toxins from the alcohol. If you put more toxins into it (i.e. greasy bacon or a Bloody Mary), you're making it work double-time to break down even more shit and get you back to normal. Now that's not a very nice way to treat yourself, is it?

So how do you get back to normal in the healthiest, most nourishing way possible? My ultimate healthy hangover fix is a banana. I swear by them, and there is research to back it up. Bananas are packed with potassium so they replenish the body of what was lost after a night of partying. They are also full of electrolytes so they'll help hydrate you. Bonus: they only have about 100 calories and they are super nutritious, as opposed to that gross plate of fries you are probably craving.

Next up on my list is fresh-squeezed orange juice. Hold the champagne. I know, I know, mimosas seem like the right choice the morning after, and they do compliment brunch quite nicely, but that whole "hair of the dog" thing is a myth. If you continue to drink, you're only adding more toxins to your body, which will slow down your recovery process and make that hangover last even longer. Try having a glass of OJ (put it in a fancy champagne flute if that makes you happy). The fructose (or sugar) in the juice will boost your energy naturally and increase the rate at which your body breaks down the toxins, so you'll feel better faster. You'll also replenish your body of all the vitamins and nutrients you lost from the night before.

And this one may seem obvious, but coffee does help. A cup or two (with water in between – remember you're still dehydrated), can restore brain function and lift that fog so you can get on with your day and actually be able to form coherent sentences.

If you're planning to tackle your hangover hiding behind a giant pair of sunglasses at brunch (my preferred method), opt for a half-white/half-yolk veggie omelet. Don't be tempted to order up pancakes or bacon. Eggs are packed with something called cysteine, which helps get rid of the toxins from all of the booze in your system. Plus, the protein will fill you up and cure that pit-of-your-stomach starvation feeling that inevitably follows a big night out.

But remember: everything in moderation, even our beloved champagne. We're all going to have a wild night every now and then, but if you can learn to respect your body, it'll happen a lot less. Appreciate and love your booze the way I've taught you to appreciate and love your food. Savor each sip. Drink slowly, and responsibly. Because nobody ever looks good fat and drunk.

Champagne Diet Manifesto

I enjoy and savor a glass of champagne whenever I want one.
I do not deprive myself of the things I love.

CHAPTER FIVE

Ditch the "Dead Weight":
Why Stress Will Make You Fat and Miserable

It's a fact: in life, we all experience stress. There are highs and lows, and most often, those lows feel a hell of a lot better when you're going through them with a box of cookies by your side. Am I right?

Although we can't change the fact that stress exists, we can change how we react to it. By learning to manage our anxiety (sans cookies), we can lower our blood pressure, lose weight, and ultimately improve our well-being.

I don't know about you, but if I look back to the most stressful times in my life, my weight was out of whack while I was going through each situation. And more often than not, I was overweight. If I had a penny for every time I wished I'd be one of those people that lost weight during my darkest days, I'd be a millionaire. But alas, the fat seems to stick to me like glue when I'm stressed out, and eating healthy is the last thing I'm thinking about.

When I started following *The Champagne Diet*, ditching the "dead weight" was just as important as introducing healthy foods into my life. This meant getting rid of all the bullshit that wasn't serving me anymore. Bad friends, unhealthy relationships, and a job that was literally draining any bit of happiness from me – it all had to go. And once I had the balls to cut those things out of my life, my relationship with food changed dramatically.

When I started following my *Champagne Diet*, ditching the "dead weight" was just as important as introducing healthy foods into my life. This meant getting rid of all the bullshit that wasn't serving me anymore. Bad friends, unhealthy relationships, and a job that was literally draining any bit of happiness from me – it all had to go.

Turning to food in times of stress is not necessarily completely our fault, however. When we're under an extreme amount of stress, our bodies produce high levels of a hormone called Cortisol, which is responsible for making us crave both salty and sweet foods. I know that the second my world starts to feel unbalanced I want to dive head first into a bag of potato chips. We've all got our vices. The trick is being aware and replacing that bad habit with something more nourishing like a bubble bath or a mini massage.

So how do we manage stress and avoid eating our feelings in the form of a giant plate of Lo Mein? Well, the first step is being aware of when it happens. For the next two weeks, I want you to keep a journal with you at all times. Every time you eat a meal, jot down two things: first, your mood, and second, what you ate. For example: *It's Tuesday afternoon and I'm feeling really energized. I just ate a big salad.* Or: *It's Friday morning, I'm so exhausted and worn out, and I just had a bagel with cream cheese.* As you go through this exercise, pay close attention to the connection between your emotional state and what you're putting in your mouth. I can guarantee you there is a connection every single time.

There are ways to self-correct our emotional eating, as well. When you feel like you're getting stressed and there's a slim chance you'll fling a dinner plate across the room or eat an entire pint of ice cream, try some of the following stress-management techniques to calm down. It will save your china as well as some unwanted calories.

The first and most obvious step is to breathe. Seriously, taking a few deep breaths in any stressful or anxiety-producing situation can do wonders for you. Getting more oxygen into your system is an instant stress-relief technique and you can do this anywhere: the office, at home, in the car, etc.

The next step is to reframe your situation. Sometimes we're so wrapped up in our crises that no matter how big or small they are we feel like the world is ending. Aside from going back to the questions in Chapter One (ex: "Am I going to die?"), you can also take a minute to slap yourself into a reality and remember that it's not necessarily always *that* bad. Try to step outside of yourself for a moment as you step away from the chips and look at your situation from another perspective. Giving yourself that space to think for a moment will help you chill out and realize that you don't need to comfort yourself with food.

And of course, the best way to avoid stress-induced meltdowns is to be proactive about managing potential stressors. The more you can design a world that is filled with healthy, nutritious foods and calming rituals, the more you will master a sense of calm and balance in your life. Things like a weekly yoga class, regular meditation, and time spent outdoors will set the tone for a healthy mindset so you can handle whatever comes your way.

Detoxing Your Life

Most of the stress in our lives comes from outside sources. Whether it is a job you're miserable in, a toxic relationship, financial issues, or health problems, there are ways to avoid eating yourself into oblivion when the shit starts to hit the fan. By taking a good, hard look at your life and all of the circumstances surrounding it, you'll be able to identify the major stressors and what you can do about them.

Right now, I want you to list the top five energy drainers in your life:

1. _____
2. _____
3. _____
4. _____
5. _____

Now, I want you take a look at that list and figure out what can be eliminated. This doesn't have to happen overnight, but you need to realize you can ultimately control every aspect of your life. And if you don't believe that, then stop reading this book right now because you're wasting your time. You must empower yourself with the belief that your life is in your control. And if there's a situation you can't change, you can absolutely change the way you respond to it. For example, not eating an entire box of Entenmann's chocolate frosted doughnuts every time you have to see your in-laws.

What stressful areas of your life can you work on eliminating or changing?

1. _____
2. _____
3. _____
4. _____
5. _____

What stressful areas of your life can you change your attitude toward?

1. _____

2. _____

3. _____

4. _____

5. _____

Understanding your cause of stress and anxiety will do wonders for your well-being and overall sense of self. Often times we turn to food when dealing with our problems head-on seems all too overwhelming. Then we wonder why we can't zip up our jeans. Start dealing with your shit and watch your mind and body shift.

Soul Food

Think about the way you feel when you eat a few slices of greasy pizza or a bag of potato chips. You probably feel run down, sluggish, and gross. The things we put into our body have both short and long-term effects on us. That pizza not only makes you feel disgusting in the moment, but if you eat enough of it, it'll cause you to pack on the pounds and you'll wind up feeling even more disgusting weeks or months down the line.

The same goes for the things we put into our soul. Our spirits need to be nourished with healthy words, encouragement, and support, just like our bodies need to be nourished with healthy foods. If you keep feeding your soul crap, you're going to feel like crap. You'll become drained and sluggish, just like you would if you ate greasy pizza every day.

Our spirits need to be nourished with healthy words, encouragement, and support, just like our bodies need to be nourished with healthy foods. If you keep feeding your soul crap, you're going to feel like crap.

When you think about the people, jobs, and environment you choose, be sure that you are surrounding yourself with the best of the best. Whether it's turning your home into a gorgeous Zen sanctuary, or working in a job that fulfills you, it's up to you to make your world beautiful. Create your "Champagne Life" from the inside out. Indulge your body and soul with the highest quality things life has to offer. There is no time for garbage on *The Champagne Diet*!

Are You Attracting Toxicity?

Although much of our stress does come from the outside, there are a handful of us who tend to invite drama and toxicity into our lives without even realizing it. Most of the time we do this with the best intentions— thinking we can fix someone, or thinking that we're just being a good friend. But if you find yourself in the middle of drama again and again, it's time to take a look inward and find out if you're inadvertently attracting the madness into your world.

I know I personally suffered from this for many years, and it's because I was a people pleaser to the core. I loved making everyone happy, and for the longest time, I thought I could fix everyone's problems. My phone was like a hotline where I gave out advice regularly and listened to my friends rattle on and on about their issues. Little did I know I was soaking up all their negativity and it was impacting me in a really, really powerful way. I was taking on *their* stress and making it a part of my own. And how did I deal with it all? You guessed it! I ate my way through.

I remember one friend, in particular, who really got to me. As soon as I'd see her number appear on my phone, I'd immediately reach for a glass of wine and then mute her while I ate popcorn as she bitched and vented. Because she never let me get a word in edgewise, she didn't even notice I was muted. Toxic people rarely notice much other than themselves. Her calls wound up adding toxicity to my world and to my body. Ultimately I got a grip on the situation and realized how negative she was, and I distanced myself from her. My brain and my ass thanked me.

So how do you know if you're attracting toxicity or if you're just being a good friend? Ask yourself these questions: Do you always pick up the phone regardless of what time that toxic person is calling? Do you feel restless when nobody "needs" you for a few days or weeks? Do you get a serious sense of satisfaction when you feel like you've "fixed" someone's problem, even temporarily?

If you've answered yes to any of these, it's time to get a new hobby, sister. You are a first-class toxic magnet and you are only going to wind up making yourself fatter and more miserable by dealing with all that stress. It's okay to care and it's certainly okay to listen, but please make sure you're making yourself a priority. If you need some more tips on this, check out my other book, *Sparkle*. Reforming people-pleasers is my specialty, so go read up!

Why Being Skinny Isn't the Answer

Here's a little secret: you can ditch the weight, but if you hang onto the "dead weight" life will remain exactly the same. Just because you successfully shed pounds does not mean you're going to have a happy, perfect life. It's so important to pay just as much attention to what you're putting in your body as to what you're letting in your world.

I once knew a woman who was in an emotionally abusive relationship. We'll call her Jess. Her boyfriend constantly ridiculed Jess for her weight, making comments to her constantly and eventually threatening to break up with her if she didn't lose thirty pounds. He brainwashed her into thinking she was ugly, unattractive, and unworthy of a healthy, happy relationship. So what did Jess do? She lost those thirty pounds. Unfortunately, she didn't lose him. She stayed in the emotionally abusive relationship and her boyfriend quickly found a new thing to pick on. His new obsession became the fact that she wasn't "toned" enough, so he mocked her constantly and bullied her into working out like a maniac to tighten up. If she had lost the thirty pounds for herself, and had the confidence to know she was a beautiful woman no matter what she weighed, she'd had moved on from Mr. Asshole a long time ago and found someone who loved her for her.

Being skinny is not the answer ladies. Being happy is. The weight will come off the way it should, in time, when you can look at your life and realize that you deserve only the best.

Champagne Diet Manifesto

I eliminate the things in life that do not serve me.
I feed my body and soul with only the best.

CHAPTER SIX
Self-Compassion Can Save Your Waistline

Think about last time you looked in the mirror and said, "*Damn*, I look good." Was it last month? Last week? Last year? Never?

Now, think about last time you looked in the mirror and said, "God, I am so fat!" I can bet my next paycheck that you've thought, or said that last statement out loud, at least once in the past week (if not more).

I don't know about you, but I have gone on total self-hating benders. Like full-on, "OMG, I AM HUGE" crying fits that leave piles upon piles of clothes all over my bedroom floor and mascara streaming down my cheeks. And those fits are usually followed by an enormous bagel with cream cheese.

Have you been there as well? You've had a really, really rough week. You're stressed out and exhausted, so you decide to reward yourself with a night out with your girlfriends. You pick your favorite restaurant, and get all decked out for a night on the town. Then, *it happens*. The moment you step into the restaurant, you lose all control. Before you know it, you've polished off an entire bread basket and two glasses of wine before you've even ordered your appetizers. You wind up eating and drinking way more than you would have liked to, and the next day you literally obsess over it. You call yourself fat all day long, you start mentally adding up all the calories you consumed, and you wind up overeating again because you think, "What's the point?"

So why do we keep at it? Why is it so hard to be good to ourselves? Why can't we just allow ourselves a break sometimes? Why can't we wake up that next day and say, "You had such a long week, you deserve a massage today. Don't worry about everything you ate last night, you're human! Let's eat really well today and start fresh."

It all starts in our childhood. We are taught from a young age to be modest, and that those who speak highly of themselves are conceited, or narcissistic. But if we don't feel good about ourselves, how will we believe anyone else? The practice of negative self-talk affects the relationships we have with ourselves, the relationships we have with lovers, friends, and the way we present ourselves to the world. Ultimately, that negativity can be responsible for the way our entire lives are shaped.

The practice of negative self-talk affects the relationships
we have with ourselves, the relationships we have with lovers,
friends, and the way we present ourselves to the world.
Ultimately, that negativity can be responsible for
the way our entire lives are shaped.

And being good to yourself has more benefits than you may realize. In a recent study posted in *The New York Times*, researchers found that there were tremendous health benefits for people who go easy on themselves. "The research suggests that giving ourselves a break and accepting our imperfections may be the first step toward better health. People who score high on tests of self-compassion have less depression and anxiety, and tend to be happier and more optimistic. Preliminary data suggest that self-compassion can even influence how much we eat and may help some people lose weight."

So how do we fix it? It's all about shifting the focus. Instead of obsessing over our so-called flaws, we need to celebrate what's right.

Write down five things you love about yourself. Remember: nobody has to see this list except you, so get your bragging on, sister!

1. _____
2. _____
3. _____
4. _____
5. _____

Forgive and Forget

What if I told you that all those times you "cheated" and over-indulged were actually good things? What if I told you that it was completely okay that you inhaled an entire bean burrito during a 3-minute commercial break for *The Bachelor* – in fact, it was necessary? Now before you think I'm totally insane, hear me out. When we eat too much, or drink too much, we're actually giving ourselves exactly what we need in that moment: comfort. No matter what your motivation is for going to town on a bag of Kettle Chips, or sucking down six glasses of Pinot Grigio at lightning speed, your body needed it; and you allowed yourself to have it. That is a great thing.

The real problem occurs afterward. The real problem occurs with the way we treat ourselves after we overeat, or overdrink: the nasty, negative self-talk, the name-calling, and the abuse. That is where the real damage is done. I know you're not eating like an animal every night. Or else you wouldn't even be reading this book. So what we need to work on is you forgiving yourself for going ape shit on that plate of Chinese food. Because it happened. And guess what? It might happen again. The sooner you can move past it each time, the sooner you can get back on track. And the less likely it is to happen again because this time you'll actually be treating yourself like a worthy human being.

The other important thing to realize is that our bodies are going to crave comfort constantly. We all work and deal with stress, and we deserve to pamper ourselves after a long day. As soon as you can identify when you're looking for a way to comfort yourself, you can start to replace those six glasses of Pinot with something a little more nourishing, like the fantastic rituals we talked about in Chapter Three. It's all about self-awareness and having the tools to replace those crappy behaviors with healthy ones.

Treat Yourself Like You Treat Your Best Friend

A few months ago, I woke up in the middle of the night to get a glass of water. I was so tired that I forgot to close the refrigerator door all the way. When I woke up in the morning and realized all our food had spoiled, I proceeded to berate myself. "Are you a moron? How could you do this? What is wrong with you?" I yelled out loud.

The way I spoke to myself bothered me for weeks. I was so disappointed by the way I lost control and how mean I was to myself. I thought about how I would have talked to my best friend if she had told me the same story. I probably would have felt so sad for her, and said something along the lines of "You poor thing! You must have been so exhausted. You really need to take better care of yourself and get more rest." So why couldn't I do this for myself?

Negative self-talk is so detrimental to our self-esteem, no matter how insignificant it may seem. We're so used to calling ourselves stupid, fat, dumb, and a host of other names that after a while, we begin to believe it. Even if it's not obvious, it becomes ingrained in us. Soon, our self-worth goes down the drain. We don't feel we deserve things like good, healthy food and a good, healthy life. I really try to catch myself, especially when I use the word "fat." Even in a seemingly harmless way, the word is horrible. I have a rule with myself, that when I catch myself calling myself fat, I have to think of something I love about myself – no matter what it is.

Write down three power phrases you can say to yourself the next time negative self-talk creeps in. Think of something positive that you can point out about yourself to counteract the insult. For example, instead of "I look so fat!" replace it with "I have an awesome ass."

1. _____

2. _____

3. _____

Build a Self-Esteem Routine

When we disrespect ourselves with our words, we usually treat ourselves in the same vein. Things like self-care go out the window, because we don't believe we deserve to look and feel good. Whenever I've been in a rut, not eating well and not treating myself well, all of my routines suffer. I stop getting my hair and nails done, I stop shopping for cute clothes, and I stop working out.

It is so vital to build a self-esteem routine into our lives. When you stop doing things that feel good, you're punishing yourself and it spirals quickly. *The Champagne Diet* is all about indulging in the best of the best, so I'm going to have you create your own self-esteem routine to keep you sparkling. Think about the things that make you feel sexy, feminine, and glamorous and incorporate them into your every day. Maybe it's a spritz of perfume before bed, or putting on makeup for even the most mundane tasks like food shopping. Perhaps it's cooking yourself a meal while sipping on a glass of bubbly, or writing in your journal. Whatever it is that makes you feel good, build it into your everyday so that you keep your glam vibration high. Because when we start to give up on these things, our health and wellness suffer – big time.

The Champagne Diet is all about indulging in the best of the best, so I'm going to have you create your own self-esteem routine to keep you sparkling. Think about the things that make you feel sexy, feminine, and glamorous, and incorporate them into your everyday.

And it's not just about perfume and pedicures. Things like getting an adequate amount of sleep are so essential for maintaining a healthy body especially if you are trying to lose weight. If you aren't sleeping well (that means getting a good, solid night's sleep without disruption) you're preventing yourself from shedding the excess pounds that you're working so hard during the day to take off. Research shows that lack of sleep can increase the presence of the hormones leptin and ghrelin. Doctors say that both can influence our appetite, and studies show that production of both may be influenced by how much or how little we sleep. The two work hand in hand as a "checks and balances" system in your body to keep your appetite in check and control feelings of hunger and fullness. When you don't get enough sleep, it drives leptin levels down, which means you don't feel as satisfied after you eat. Lack of sleep causes ghrelin levels to rise, which means your appetite is stimulated, so you want to eat more.

Bet you never realized beauty sleep was so important, huh? So don't feel guilty the next time you decide to turn in early for the night or sleep in a little late on the weekends. Your body needs it.

Create three things you can do for yourself this week that will make you feel like a queen (remember, sleep counts!)

1. _____

2. _____

3. _____

Champagne Diet Manifesto

I treat myself the way I would treat my best friend with kind, loving words of encouragement and support, always.

CHAPTER SEVEN
Love the Skin You're In

Can we get one thing straight? All women are beautiful. All bodies are beautiful. Curvy is not sexier than skinny. Skinny is not sexier than curvy. We're all gorgeous, feminine creatures that deserve to celebrate the skin we're in – no matter what shape or size we are.

In 2012, I wrote an article for *The Huffington Post* titled *Curvy vs. Skinny: Let's End the Women's Weight Wars Once and For All*. In the article, I called out all of the posts we see all over Facebook, Instagram, and Pinterest pitting skinny women against curvy women. I know you've seen them, too— the pictures of voluptuous women, showing off their curves with big, bold words printed across them that say things like "Real women have curves." I take issue with this for a few reasons. Yes, real women do have curves. And they are also thin, heavy, bony, chunky and everything in between. It's completely and totally unacceptable to claim a woman isn't a "real" woman because of her size. Nobody is better than anyone else. We've got to stop bullying others in an effort to raise our own self-esteem.

It also worries me that we're *still* having this conversation. And I'm *still* writing about it. There were hundreds and hundreds of comments underneath my article of people debating my stance. Some felt that I was ignoring the obesity issue. Others felt I was right on target in my message of body confidence and acceptance of all body types. It means that there is still a lot of work to do not only in the media, but also within ourselves when it comes to obsessing over women's weight. Don't get me wrong, obesity is a real epidemic and should be addressed. I am in no way saying that you should ignore good health and be okay with being overweight if you are unhealthy. You should absolutely consult your doctor if you are concerned about your weight and work out a plan to be your best, healthiest self. But that is your business, and nobody else's. It's just not okay for anyone else to meddle in that very personal issue, especially in a public forum.

When it comes to body confidence, however, it is crucial that we celebrate our size no matter what – even if (especially if) we are overweight. You may be thinking: "There's no way I can be happy at this size! I'm miserable!" And I get it. I've been there. But that is precisely the time you need to have self-compassion and accept the place you're in, because the longer you beat yourself up and stress out about your weight, the longer it will take to get you to a place where you can take control of your health and start making positive changes.

Appreciating Your Beautiful Body

When I listen to women trash-talk their bodies because of the way they look, I can't help but cringe. Not only because I feel so bad that they are suffering so deeply, but also because I want them to realize just how amazing their bodies are. Think about all of the things your body does for you every single day: your lungs pull in air to help you breath, your heart beats, your brain and entire nervous system keep you thinking, speaking and feeling. Your body is a well-oiled machine that runs all on its own. So why do you hate it so much?

Appreciating all that your body does for you every day is something we need to remind ourselves to do constantly. Just like we have our gratitude ritual for all the things in our lives (if you don't have a gratitude ritual, you need to get on that!) you should also give thanks every single day for your body. Be grateful for your eyes that are reading this book right now, be grateful for your heart that beats strong and allowed you to wake up this morning. Be grateful for your legs that allow you to get up and walk across the room, and be grateful for your ears that allow you to hear your children laugh, or listen to your favorite songs. I know I probably sound a little woo woo right now, but this stuff holds serious meaning. Practicing gratitude for your body every single day will help you understand that our bodies serve such a bigger purpose than the way they look. This is a key principle on *The Champagne Diet*, so feel free to write it down on a hot pink post-it if you have to and put it somewhere you will see every day.

Make a list of five things you are grateful for that your body does for you:

1. _____
2. _____
3. _____
4. _____
5. _____

Think about all of the things your body does for you every single day: your lungs pull in air to help you breath, your heart beats, your brain and entire nervous system keep you thinking, speaking and feeling. Your body is a well-oiled machine that runs all on its own. So why do you hate it so much?

Why You Should Break Up With the Scale
(At Least Temporarily)

I will be the first to admit that I have had an extremely unstable relationship with the scale. I'd even go so far as to call it borderline obsession. There was a point where I was weighing myself up to five times a day. Five times a day! That is totally insane. And the worst part was, each time the scale shifted, I freaked out. I obsessed over why I didn't immediately drop pounds after going for a long, sweaty run. Or why I could eat nothing but a banana all day, and be up two pounds before bed. Can you say dysfunction?

Eventually, I got things under control and my relationship with the scale has improved dramatically. Mainly because I now understand how and why our weight is constantly fluctuating. Sodium is one of the biggest culprits for what seems like a weight "gain." If you've indulged in a little too much salt, you should know that you will retain water. Two sixteen-ounce glasses of water are equal to a pound. So if you spent the night gorging on pub food, and you guzzled a few extra glasses of water before bed, there's your answer. But don't be afraid of water if you're bloated. Drink even more so that you can properly flush out your system. And here's my golden trick: eat a banana. Bananas have natural diuretic properties so you'll get rid of the bloat even faster.

Another reason the scale may be driving you insane is because you've been eating too many carbs. Your body can store up to 500 grams, which can show up when you weigh in because that means you're storing water, too. If you're overloading on carbs, try to cut back a little bit, but not completely. Focus on eating rich, nutrient-dense carbs like whole grains in the form of brown rice, quinoa, etc. and eat a small amount at each meal. Ditch the refined carbs like white bread and pasta.

So stop obsessing over the numbers and realize that your

body is dynamic and always in flux. Remember what I said about your emotions being your weight-loss barometer? Stick to that. You'll know inherently if you're eating well. And when you eat well, you feel great. If you're a scale-a-holic, I challenge you to take a break for an extended period of time; whatever makes sense to you. Whether it's two weeks or one week, take a break so you can regain some of your sanity.

Does Size Matter?

One of the most frustrating misconceptions surrounding weight is that skinny automatically equals healthy, and heavier automatically means unhealthy. There are plenty of thin people who are severely unhealthy, and there are plenty of women who are heavier but are extremely healthy and fit. It is your responsibility to control your own health and wellness. Nobody knows your body like you do. You know what you put in your body every day, and you know when you're getting enough exercise.

When I was in my early 20's, I was extremely stressed out and unhealthy. I was eating fast-food at least a few times a week, I was in and out of toxic relationships, I was double-fisting vodka cranberries all weekend long with my friends, staying up until 4 am and partying like it was my side job. Quite frankly, I had no idea how I made it to the gym, but somehow I managed to work out on a pretty regular basis, and it was all for vanity. I lived off diet soda and I bounced from diet to diet, constantly losing and gaining weight. My health was clearly not a priority.

Fast forward to today, I am healthier and more grounded than I've ever been. But I'm also about fifteen pounds heavier that I used to be. I eat a mainly organic, vegetarian diet, I meditate, I enjoy wine and champagne in moderation, and I exercise. Why am I heavier than I was ten years ago? I really couldn't give you a valid answer, other than the fact that my metabolism is slower and I live a relatively calm, happy life (no more days of starvation while fighting with boyfriends). Maybe the stress isn't eating me alive. Who knows, but it's something I've made peace with, because as I keep saying, my emotions have become my weight-loss barometer.

I'll be honest, though; it took time to get here. At first, I found myself obsessing over the numbers on the scale. I was so frustrated with the fact that no matter what I did, I just couldn't seem to lose more weight. But once I came to accept the fact that my life was so much better than it was ten years ago, it all clicked. I learned to place value on the things that mattered: I was married to a wonderful man who adored me; I was successful in my career; I had wonderful friends and family; and I was truly and deeply happy. Once I began to shift my focus to the things that mattered, the number on the scale became less and less important.

Once I began to shift my focus to the things that mattered,
the number on the scale became less and less important.

Make a list of three personal accomplishments that have nothing to do with your weight:

1. _____
2. _____
3. _____

It's so important to remind ourselves of all of the kick-ass, phenomenal things we've done, and continue to do in our lives. We are gorgeous, successful, creative, intelligent creatures and it's about time we started celebrating that. Who's with me?

Champagne Diet Manifesto

I love and I appreciate my body and all of the amazing things
it does for me. I celebrate all the things I've accomplished.

CHAPTER EIGHT
Get Your Sexy On

Oscar de la Renta once said, "You have to walk like you have three men walking behind you." I love this quote for so many reasons. It's playful, it's feminine, and it's all about confidence. When you strut your stuff, you just feel better. And chances are, you stand up straighter and suck in that gut, too. When you are paying attention to the way you look and feel, you eat better and treat your body better. It just works.

Ask any man what he finds sexiest about a woman and he will tell you this: confidence. When we feel good, we look good. There is no amount of makeup, perfume, or lingerie that will make you more attractive than really believing you are one hot mama. All of those things help, but you've gotta believe it first. But is it possible to look and feel sexy when you're ten, twenty, or even fifty pounds overweight? Abso-fucking-lutely. And in this chapter, I'm going to show you how.

"You have to walk like you have three
men walking behind you."
- Oscar de la Renta

In the past when I've been at a weight that was not ideal for me, I tortured myself over it. Whether it was depriving myself of good food and wine, or taking complete shopping hiatuses, or even giving up on my routine blonde highlights and walking around with three inch roots, I shut down all forms of pampering when I was on a mission to lose weight. I even stopped wearing my lacy push-up bras and switched to sports bras. I *know*, so bad.

In retrospect, this was the precise time I should have been pampering myself, because I clearly needed as much love as possible. And by neglecting my self-care, I was turning to food to fill that void. I felt gross, so I just ate more. It was a miserable downward spiral that took away any and all hope and confidence that things would get better. Can you relate?

Dress the Part

During those times, I never felt like I could pull off a "sexy" look. I just felt like a frumpy, unattractive mess. The odd thing is, when I looked at other fuller-figured girls, some even carrying around a little extra weight who dressed well and looked put together I'd think, "She's got it going on!" I seemed to be so much more accepting of everyone else but myself. Why was I beating myself up over an extra fifteen pounds when I saw no problem with a girl who may have been thirty pounds overweight? It had nothing to do with size and everything to do with confidence.

I remember the day it clicked for me. I had been married for about a year, and had gained close to twenty pounds. Twenty fucking pounds. I was overworked and adjusting to married life (nobody tells you that the first year is one of the hardest years of your life), and in short, I was a total stress case. I couldn't figure out how to balance it all. I was making no time for myself. Crappy food was becoming my ally again and I had zero motivation to move, let alone workout. I decided I was over living in Old Navy trapeze tops (you know those billowing shirts that make you look pregnant, but you wear them anyway because you'd rather look huge than have someone see an actual fat roll?). I knew I needed to do something to snap myself out of my funk. I knew eating better and moving was the answer, but I needed some motivation to get me back in the right mindset where I felt like I deserved to look good again.

That night, I left work an hour early and I took out $300 in cash from the ATM. I told myself I had to spend all $300 on clothes and accessories that made me feel amazing. I called my husband and warned him I'd be home late. In the back of my head I panicked that I'd come home with more trapeze shirts, but I made a promise to myself that I was going to shop till I dropped and end up with a new wardrobe that made me feel nothing less than fabulous. If I looked great, I'd feel great, and that would inspire me to start respecting my body again and nourishing it with all of the right foods.

Before my shopping spree, I went to The Empire Room, a bar/lounge at the bottom level of The Empire State Building. I found a seat at the bar and ordered myself a glass of champagne. I had been married at the Empire State Building, and the whole vibe of the building represented the epitome of romantic glamour to me. The Empire Room is one of my favorite bars; it's sultry, sexy, and has an art deco flair. It was the perfect environment to get in the right state of mind if I was going to embark on what seemed like *Mission Impossible*. When the bartender served my crisp glass of bubbles, I silently toasted myself. I literally said in my head, "You deserve to look and feel as beautiful as you did on your wedding day, always." I remember feeling so luminous and radiant on that day and I refused to become a fat, miserable wife who had given up on herself. It was time to slam on the breaks – quickly.

I sipped on my champagne while I worked up the nerve to

enter the Macy's dressing rooms, and about twenty minutes later, I was ready to tackle *Operation Get Hot Again*. The bubbly definitely helped me relax a bit and stop obsessing over what size jeans I was trying on, and before I knew it I was actually trying things on and – gasp – liking the way I looked! I discovered a few new stores I had never set foot into before, and even asked the sales girls for help. "What do you think would look good on me?" was a question I never dreamed I'd ask another person, especially a size-two sales girl. But believe it or not, I wound up with some really great recommendations and worked up the courage to try things on I never thought I could pull off.

Blame it on the champers or the fact that I chose to have a positive mindset that night, but I spent every last penny on myself and returned home with a gorgeous new wardrobe including cute blazers, sexy new bras, pants that actually fit and looked great, new shoes, and tons of accessories. I decided that next weekend that I was going to give my closet a major overhaul and donate anything I did not feel 100% amazing in. Seven garbage bags later, my clothes were whittled down to nearly nothing aside from the few things I picked up for myself during my *Operation Get Hot Again* shopping spree, but I was thrilled to have clothes that I looked and felt awesome in.

Oh, and here's an expert tip: do not be cheap with yourself! Now is not the time to buy crappy, inexpensive garbage. Invest in beautiful fabrics that flatter your figure. And please, don't get hung up on sizes. Nothing will make you feel fatter than too-tight clothing. Buy items you can breathe in. Both Michael Kors and Vince Camuto make fantastic plus-sized lines, as do many other designers. In fact, stores like Nordstrom and Bloomingdales have entire plus-sized collections filled with beautiful styles from top-of-the-line designers. Treat yourself to only the best. You're on *The Champagne Diet*, remember?

Girl Power

Many of us tend to lose our feminine flair when we're unhappy with our weight. I know that when I was overweight, the last thing I wanted to do was put on lipstick or get my hair blown out. Instead, I wanted to hide every last inch of my body in sweats and remain indoors as much as possible. And heels? Out of the question! I lived in my running sneakers and Uggs at all times.

But it is so important to harness your feminine energy regardless of what size you are. Being a girl is fun! Tapping into your womanly essence is one of the quickest ways to boost your confidence and feel sexy. Whether it's getting a pedicure, or a luxurious massage, or buying new makeup, don't forget to do something at least once a week that allows you to indulge in a little girly time.

Tapping into your womanly essence is one of the
quickest ways to boost your confidence and feel sexy.

And it's not just about the way we dress. Being feminine can mean so many things. One of my favorite girly things to do is buy fresh flowers. I love putting gorgeous floral arrangements around my apartment, especially in the kitchen. I also love to cook a beautiful meal while sipping on a glass of wine. I put on my Frank Sinatra station on Pandora, pour a glass of red, and let my kitchen fill up with the aroma of whatever I'm making. I'm totally in my element in that moment and I feel like one hell of a sexy, beautiful woman while doing it. So what makes *you* feel girly?

Make a list of three things you can do to feel feminine:

1. _____
2. _____
3. _____

Flirt, Flirt, Flirt!

Whether you're single, married, in a relationship, whatever – you should never, ever stop flirting. Flirting is a core essential part of who we are as women. And by flirting, I don't mean hitting on tons of guys at bars and handing out your number (unless of course, that's your goal – no judgment!). But something as simple as smiling at someone in the elevator, or making small talk with the guy who is making your coffee can spark that little sex flame that may be lying dormant in you for whatever reason. Maybe you've been married for a while and feeling like no other man on Earth besides your husband finds you attractive anymore. Maybe you've put on weight after your baby and you think guys now only look at you as a fat mom. Well you could not be more wrong, darling. Men *love* women. And they love to be flirted with. I can guarantee that no matter how hot you think you are a man will think you're even hotter. If you giggle or run your fingers through your hair, he *will* flirt back, and you'll wind up feeling like sex on a stick instantly. Trust me.

So how does flirting fit into being healthy? Well, as I've been drilling into your brain during this entire book, when we feel good about ourselves and our bodies, we treat ourselves the way we should. Our emotional motives for overeating are what destroy us. It's not about having the will power to say no to that cake. It's not about counting the calories. It's on us to develop an innate sense of confidence and self-love so that we naturally make smarter food choices for the rest of our lives. And sometimes, we can't build that confidence alone. So doll yourself up and get out there and work your girly magic. The boys are waiting for you.

Oh, and if you're in a relationship or have a booty call, friend with benefits, whatever, do not stop having sex. Shutting things down in the bedroom is the quickest way to get fat and miserable. Buy some figure-flattering lingerie, do it by candlelight, whatever it takes to get you back on your back with your partner. I can't tell you how many women (including myself), basically turned into a nun because we felt overweight and unattractive. You know what that does to you? It makes you feel like a gross, unwanted, unsexy frump. So push those insecurities to the side and get on the next train for Penisville. And don't forget sex burns calories, too. All aboard!

Shutting things down in the bedroom is the
quickest way to get fat and miserable.

So let's recap, my sexy little vixens. In order to live *The Champagne Diet* and be your healthiest, happiest, hottest self, you've got to get your sexy on. So stop waiting to buy clothes until you lose the weight. Buy them now. Wear what feels good. Put on makeup every day (at the very least, a little blush and lip gloss). Do your hair. Shower with luxurious bath gels. Cook a gorgeous dinner in a pretty, ruffled apron. Buy fresh flowers. Wear sexy underwear. Smile at the UPS guy. The more glamour and sex appeal we can add to our lives, the more feminine we will feel. And the more feminine we feel, the better we'll treat our bodies. Harness your feminine energy, and remember to have fun with it. Looking great at any size builds confidence, and you can't get much hotter than that.

Champagne Diet Manifesto

I harness my feminine energy always.
I relish in the joy that is being a girl.

CHAPTER NINE
Get Moving

You didn't think we were going to get through this book without talking about working out, did you? I know, I know. It's a pain in the ass. You have no time. You hurt your calf last month and feel like you can't do anything in the gym. You work too much. You hate to sweat. These are all of the excuses that I am all too familiar with because I've made them myself. But you know what? Unless we're got our ass-ets in motion, it's going to be a hell of a lot harder to think straight, lose weight, and live a healthy life (and stare at your naked ass in the mirror).

Working out does not have to be torture. In fact, for a very long time, I believed it did. I'd punish myself with rigorous work-outs like five-mile runs at 6 AM just to prove to myself that I could do it. I thought I had to kill myself in the gym to reap any of the benefits of working out. I thought I wasn't "fit enough" until I could upload a Facebook profile photo of me wearing a marathon number. It's still a goal, but for different reasons now.

Let's get something straight: working out won't work for you until you have fun with it and accept that it has to be a part of your life in some way, shape, or form. This isn't rocket science or some genius concept; it's just the simple truth. When we approach working out as something we have to do to "pay for our sins" we immediately zap our motivation. I don't know about you, but punishment and self-hate gets me nowhere. Why are we so convinced that it has to suck?

Everything Counts

One of my colleagues actually feels guilty when she works out. She claims that she has so much fun working out that it feels like play, and she has to limit her time spent engaging in physical activity because she feels badly that it takes her away from her work. I remember when she first told me this I assumed she was lying to me. There was no way in hell anyone could actually feel guilty for having too much fun working out. Was she out of her damn mind? But when she began explaining to me all the things she did to exercise, I got it. She didn't spend hours doing boring workouts; instead, she got outdoors as much as possible. She spent an hour hiking with her dogs. She took long, gorgeous walks around her neighborhood. She played tennis. It's no wonder she felt like she was "cheating." She was having a frickin' blast.

Guess what else is true? Working out doesn't have to be your life's purpose. For example, I go through times in my life where it is *not* my priority to work out constantly. Sometimes it is, and during those times I am ready to go balls to the wall and challenge and push myself, and I love every minute of it. Sometimes, I'm lucky to get in a series of squats and a long walk on a good day. It's important to understand that as long as we are moving, we are doing something good for ourselves. It's essential that we keep our bodies in motion, no matter what we're doing. As the famous saying goes, "A body in motion stays in motion. A body at rest stays at rest." Because I don't have enough hours to spend in the gym at this point in my life, I make sure I walk everywhere. I'm constantly moving. If I'm home, I'm running back and forth to the store. If I'm working, I walk through the city during lunch or when I leave the office before getting on the bus to come home. Any movement is better than no movement, and walking is one of the best ways to do it.

On the flipside, I sometimes get in a zone where I really want to challenge myself. I've tried everything from bootcamp classes, to HIIT workouts, to boxing – you name it. And every single one of those times I've wanted to be there. I never force myself to do anything I don't want to. If my heart isn't in it, it's just not gonna feel good. You've got to do what excites you – what gets you motivated. So I challenge you to think of some fun and fabulous ways to keep your body in motion. Maybe it's a hip hop dance class, or a surfing lesson. Maybe you've always wanted to go horseback riding or maybe you love bowling. Whatever it is that you love to do that doesn't involve sitting still, jot it down. It *all* counts.

1. _____
2. _____
3. _____
4. _____
5. _____

Know Your Own Bullshit

Of course it's important to "do what you can" and know that everything counts, but it's also important to know when you're simply bullshitting yourself. Are you really *that* busy? *That* sore? I've gotten to a point where I know how to read my "BS meter" quite well. I have a technique where if I'm contemplating a workout, I look at the clock. Let's say I'm thinking about a thirty-minute workout. I look at the clock and imagine it being thirty minutes ahead, when my workout is done. I think about the way I'll feel when I'm finished: energized, accomplished, healthy, and confident. If that doesn't work, I go a step further. I think about all the ways I'll feel in a month after I am consistently doing my workouts. I envision my jeans fitting a little looser, my arms looking toned in a tank top. I get really honest with myself and literally talk myself into the workout. And guess what? Every single time I am thankful that I did it. Think about it: have you ever completed a workout and thought, "Shit, *that* was a bad idea." Probably not.

So the next time you're putting off a workout, allow yourself to be completely honest. Even if you still don't wind up working out, learn to read your BS meter. The more you get to know and understand your own excuses, the quicker you can work through them.

Of course it's important to "do what you can" and
know that everything counts, but it's also important to know
when you're simply bullshitting yourself.

Use it or Lose It

If all else fails, here's a quick way to motivate yourself to move: if you don't lose it, you will lose it. And I'm not just talking about your toned muscles. I'm talking about your life. I know I sound harsh and dramatic, but here me out. There are stats to back this up. As we get older, our risk for disease and death goes up drastically if we are not exercising. Millions of Americans are dying each year because they aren't exercising, and in turn, they are developing diseases like diabetes and heart disease, among others. In fact, economists have determined these deaths cost our country about three trillion dollars a year. I mean, how scary is that?

And it's only going to get harder for us as things like technology and convenience take over our worlds. A few hundred years ago, being sedentary wasn't much of a problem because people weren't parked in front of computers all day long, only to go home and heat up meals in the microwave. We moved because it was necessary for survival. Now, movement isn't really required of us the way it once was. We drive everywhere, and we work at desk jobs. That's why it's on us to be conscious of how important it is to get up off our asses as often as possible and use our bodies before we lose 'em.

Champagne Diet Manifesto

I do not view exercise as punishment or torture. I keep my beautiful body in motion because it deserves nothing less.

CHAPTER TEN
Living The Champagne Diet

So, how are you feeling? Are you ready to go out and buy a fridge full of organic fruits and veggies, a bottle of Moet, and a lacy thong? Well then I've done my job! But seriously, I want to spend this last chapter revisiting the main concepts of *The Champagne Diet* so that when I leave you, you can go out there and live your healthiest, most effervescent life. Remember, I'm not four inches and you can't keep me in your back pocket, so you're gonna have to do the work on your own after we're done here.

First things first: diets don't work. You are going to ditch the concept of "dieting" and "cheat days" and instead treat yourself like a gorgeous, worthy woman who deserves to eat real, healthy, delicious foods. You are no longer going to view food, or your body, as the enemy. You can, and will, develop a fabulously passionate relationship with yourself. You're going to harness your feminine essence and flex your flirt muscles as often as possible. You're going to eliminate all the things that no longer serve you, including (but not limited to): clothes that don't make you feel absolutely stunning, guys who can't appreciate a curve or two, people and things that drain your energy, and food that does not nourish your body. You are going to design a dream life that will become your reality. You are going to believe, with every fiber of your being, that you deserve it all.

Now, let's get back to those feelings you wrote down in Chapter One. Remember, all of those ways you wanted to feel if dieting and weight weren't an issue in your life? All of those feelings are completely and totally attainable if you just learn to channel them. Please believe that. There's no reason why anyone else in this world is entitled to feel a sense of happiness, calm, and passion and you're not. It's up to you to set the tone of your day, every day. And the number on the scale should have absolutely nothing to do with it.

Let's review our manifestos. These should be your go-to's after you're done reading this book. These quick little reminders will help you stay sane and realize just how attainable a healthy, happy lifestyle really is.

And if you want to print them out, you can go to *TheChampagneDiet.com* for a free, fancy, downloadable copy. Cause I'm all tech-savvy like that.

Champagne Diet Manifestos

I truly believe I am worthy of an amazing life. My weight does not define what I am capable of or what I deserve.

I take responsibility for my own health. I focus on health over weight-loss and accept that there is no "quick fix."

I indulge in delicious, whole foods that energize my body, mind and soul. I create nourishing rituals to restore balance and wellness in my life.

I enjoy and savor a glass of champagne whenever I want one. I do not deprive myself of the things I love.

I eliminate the things in life that do not serve me. I feed my body and soul with only the best.

I treat myself the way I would treat my best friend with kind, loving words of encouragement and support, always.

I love and I appreciate my body and all of the amazing things it does for me. I celebrate all the things I've accomplished.

I harness my feminine energy always. I relish in the joy that is being a girl.

I do not view exercise as punishment or torture. I keep my beautiful body in motion because it deserves nothing less.

Champagne has changed my life forever. It may sound crazy, but it's the truth. That one glass of bubbles that I had on that fateful night allowed me to change the way I thought about my world and myself. It has inspired a lifestyle, a brand, a business, books, and an entire following of women who all want to celebrate themselves in some way every day. It has allowed me to become a stronger, healthier, and happier person – one who has become dedicated to helping other women do the same.

I hope that you've found this book to be helpful. I hope that if you've struggled with your weight and your body image, you've now found yourself in a place where it all feels a little bit more peaceful. I hope that you've become enlightened enough to make changes to the way you eat, and realize that your body is a precious place that deserves to be respected and well preserved. And most importantly, I hope you realize how beautiful you always were, and how beautiful you always will be.

Cheers!

TOASTS OF HONOR

Mom, you've been my biggest fan from the beginning. Thank you for always loving me, laughing with me, and making me believe that anything is possible.

Ryan, you are the most loving, supportive husband a girl could ever ask for. You make me feel like the smartest, coolest, most beautiful girl every day of my life.

To my girlfriends: What would I do without you? Thank you for always understanding. For always listening. And for always making me feel like I will always be okay.

To everyone who helped me make this book a reality especially Cara Loper and Cara Lockwood, thank you so much! We've done it again.

And finally, to my Champagne Girls: thank you for continuing to read my words, believe in my dreams, and inspire me every single day.